Marie Hanna Curran

Observant Observings

Marie Hanna Curran

Observant Observings

SMOOTH STONES PRESS

AN IMPRINT OF

TAYEN LANE

PUBLISHING

Copyright

Edited by Bri Bruce
Cover Photographs courtesy Shutterstock
Cover Design Tayen Lane Design

Acknowledgments

Many thanks to all at Tayen Lane who have made my first poetry collection a reality. My words would not have made it onto these pages had it not been for the encouragement of Kermit Heartsong and Bri Bruce. Thanks must also be handed to my ever-faithful husband, whose dexterity has enhanced my ability to balance resting and writing. Thanks also to my wonderful friends and family, to the cups of tea around my kitchen table, the phone calls, texts, e-mails, and giggles at the word "author." A special word of thanks to all my followers and readers at my blog, currankentucky.wordpress.com. You have travelled part of this road with me and I thank you for lending me your eyes and your ears.

Dedication

In loving memory of my grandmother Hanna Curran

And

In dedication to those sharing couches and beds with Myalgic Encephalomyelitis on a daily basis.

Contents

Part Three

THE SEASONS

Part Four

TIME (THE PAST & PRESENT)

Part Five
PEOPLE IN SOCIAL SETTINGS

Marie Hanna Curran

Observant Observings

Part One

NATURE

Living takes many forms, bright lights, noisy streets… a green field, quiet eyes…

In Need of Witness Protection

IN NEED OF WITNESS PROTECTION

Yesterday, at approximately 4:45 p.m.,
I witnessed an attempted mass murder.

Above my head, blackbirds danced on their stage of clouds.
To my right, a wagtail moseyed along my front wall.
In front of me, ten or more birds bounced between
their peanut feeder and favoured summer greened tree.

Then from the field to my left, a sparrowhawk swooped.

The small birds ran to their tree;
his beak aimed down their middle.
The branches lifted as he moved under cover
away from my eyes. Screeches, tussles ensued.
Additional pleadings carried from neighbouring trees.

Quickly he reemerged.

Pointing my sun glasses toward him,
I searched out his beak.
Empty. I looked back to the tree.

Time changed hands…

A young farmer peddled his way up the road,
a pickaxe dangling from the back of his bike.
Two blackbirds reappeared, kites without strings,
rising higher and higher, loose bullets.
A crow stopped at the empty feeder.
No birds, no dropped peanuts.
He moved on.

Then one lone bird peered
from beneath green foliage
and flew toward the hill, away
from the attempted massacre.

As, dubiously, bird by bird,
the tree uncurled itself.

IN THIS WIND

Everything looks different in this wind.
My young trees, angled
Loose their dependability.

As do my curtains, once straight
Now billowing, large sailed
On a flamboyant ship.

Even my ears seem strange,
As if a thick-leafed forest
Sways between them.

While my feet, stuck in boots,
Remain rooted.
Yes, my feet are rooted. . . .

It's just my boots
look different
In this wind. . . .

INTACT

Fourteen steps up toward the sky
And in the spare room
Against the paned glass,
Christmas trees out of season
Trip up to my nose.

My eyes fall on two house martins
Lowering toward last year's cut grass.
Mud. Two beaks. Clay.
Back up to eye level:
Hammer and drum.

Their foundation for this year's nest
In the same place as last year.
Only that ruined, overwintered,
Like the castle at the other side
Of the Christmas trees—

Trees growing to be torn down, untacked.
And in one branch sits a cuckoo,
His summer home almost intact.

Death of a Spider

DEATH OF A SPIDER

I found a spider dead this morning,
Looking alive, but dead, beside the TV.
I wondered if he'd been watching
Something, or if his heart had stopped
Before he had his chance.

Plain Sight

PLAIN SIGHT

There were hundreds of them
Strung out across the barbed-
Wire fence. As if sculpted,
Crafted by ghosts, seen only
When the sun angled the morn,
Each white web echoing back
That first light. Illuminated,
Touched by a sun once hidden
By night. And for that moment,
Each crafted spider web
Showed itself off, like Newgrange
On the summer solstice
Before the world clocked passed dawn,
And the ghosts hid themselves
In the plainest of sight.

Labour Days

LABOUR DAYS

I watched them work
For two days.

Eight of them
Black and white birds
Over on loan from Africa.

I told Donal how they worked —
My birds I called them.

How they stuck the tiniest spots
Of damp mud to our wall,
How it dried.

How they knew
When it was strong enough
To take more mud.

How they knew how to shape it,
To turn it into a home.
And when it was done

I told Donal about their small door,
How deep the bottom seemed.
And then I sat back and wondered

What if they, those eight,
Weren't holidaying?

What if they were slaves
Brought over from Africa?

Popeye

POPEYE

He was born of a black and white mother
And an even blacker father,
The newest member of our
Holstein Friesen herd,
Popeye.

His name gifted to him because
Both eyes popped from their sockets
Like rabbits in headlights. As for his skin,
Like a baby chicken, all pink
With short fuzzy white hair.

From the moment his mother licked his back,
It was evident he was one to watch.
When spring arrived all the other
Black and white calves were turned out
In the orchard, all taught the bookwork
Of the electric fence.
Not Popeye.

He remained indoors, under fresh straw
Bathed in armed hugs,

His skin too pink, even for an Irish spring.
But when summer arrived
And the power washer ready
To clean down the barns,
Dad sent Popeye away.

No amount of arms could pull him back
From the place where they knew
How to treat such pink calves with special eyes.
Popeye...

Retired Wagtail

RETIRED WAGTAIL

He spends the day within my garden.
First facing the sun he sits,
His chest puffed, his tail
A walking stick.

Then, like an elderly farmer, he slouches
Along the weathered grey kerbing,
His head in no rush,
His feet to match.

With a gentle jump, he hops to the stone
In my driveway, picking his toes
Over moss and coloured weeds.
Wings clasped behind his back.

Later, perched atop a wooden post,
He watches, his head and tail
A metronome.

From there he sees it all: the sun, the wind,
The rain, time passed.

Violet turns Brown

VIOLET TURNS BROWN

The buds unleafed themselves,
Soft violet velvet

Like a newborn's skin,
Purple at first

And then, time past,
They grew tougher, thicker,

As if mimicking the older ones,
Their colour turned brown.

Who would have thought
It possible to start out one way

And end up something entirely different?

Shattering

SHATTERING

Beneath a galaxy,
A dangling crystal chandelier,

Pockets of miniature ice rings
Sprung up from the glacier-covered rocks.

Wooden posts licked in frosting;
Barbed wire weighed down
By stalactites.

When suddenly the chandelier
It shattered,

The ice rings cracked

One   by   one,

A frozen field in thaw.

The wooden posts

Wood
Once more.

But the stalactite
Remained,

Sharp
Barbed wire.

Part Two

EVERYDAY OBJECTS

Seeing isn't always believing. Sometimes we have to stop to truly see, to truly believe.

Seeing is Real

SEEING IS REAL

There's a bronzed statue of a branch
Behind the door in her living room.
It has eight fairy lights on its eight leaved twigs.
The branch itself is grooved
As if to make it real.

Outside her window, there are many trees,
Many branches
All within her grasp.
None of which she's seen,
But all are real.

Intensive Care

INTENSIVE CARE

It was the way she spoke of them,
A mother pointing out
Her children's personalities.

This one, ceramic, will chip.
You can throw this one in the oven,
But that one, well, its handle
Would roll into a giant ball of plastic.
Keep it where it's meant to be
Stuck to the hob.

And then her warnings,
Like a mother parting with her first born
At his first slumber party.

Never turn the heat up beyond three
The metal will separate.
As for the dishwasher;
Don't let it near. A damp cloth
That's all it needs, wipe its face
Dry it off, hang it up.
But never let it near a dishwasher,
Those things strip everything off.

Frying pans, need intensive care.

Telephone Pole

TELEPHONE POLE

Seeing sounds is make believe?

Well, looking out my windowpane,

My eyes hear voices now,

There, beyond, a phone exchange

Jutting to the sky, a simple pole

With wires of string against

The bluest sky, and so it brings

Varied voices to my dazzled eyes.

Bookworm

BOOKWORM

Books can be dangerous places.
Just last week I got lost,
Like in a game of hide and seek
When the finder loses interest
In his subject, the world lost interest in me.

I found myself drawn deep
Into the folds of another world,
All stacked just the same, yet going
Somewhere entirely different.
Like a bus stop, or train stop, I picked my route

And got lost between Saturn's rings.
There I was, a small worm, spinning
First on rings, then deeper into clusters
Of matter. It was light years before
The next spacecraft was due. Waiting,

Stars burst and planets danced
At the sun's edge, pushing and pulling
Her puppets on invisible strings.

Bathing on the axis of Enceladus, I waited
For the last craft to land.

Then, sitting at its small round window,
I wondered if scientists would ever know
Of the day a worm had visited outer space.

Electoral Canvasing - Ireland May 2014

ELECTORAL CANVASING–IRELAND MAY 2014

Overnight, lampposts,

Telegraph poles,

Wooden stakes,

Once keepers of barbed wire

And touchings of leaves,

Morphed into promises:

Words swearing

70,000 new jobs,

12,000 new classrooms,

All promising to change my world.

Some smiled,

Some leered,

One was missing a tooth,

Another a fake moustache —

Some local artist at play —

But behind the words,

The promises,

The same lampposts stood idly by.

Washing Line

WASHING LINE

Legs intertwined in shackles,
Only you upside down,
Swinging in the breath of day.

Beside you lie the casualties
Of the weekend's busy war,
Prisoners planning to escape,

The wind in ruptured chorus
Clanging at the bars.
Colours tugging on the line,

Cursing those who pinned them down,
Stopped
From roaming free.

Dancing Shoes
DANCING SHOES

I've danced in discos, late night bars,
On stage with drag queens.

I've held first love among other first loves,
I've danced both slow and tight.

I've held a hairbrush and broom,
Boogied both living room and kitchen.

I've spent time hidden in a bathroom
While Betty Bible taught the rest
Of my class how to point.

If that were today, I'd still be in that bathroom,
Or better still, here, for I'd never
Go back to that first pair of shoes.

My Aurora Borealis

MY AURORA BOREALIS

My kitchen — longitude, latitude,
Tiles facing north —
Stares down the mouth
Of a borealis source,

A mixing of gasses, white-yellow strokes
Streaking across
Years of bog turf.

Pulling my chair up close to the grate,
Greenish white lighting
Flicker my face,

When all of a sudden, the fire turns to ash
Leaving a chimney
Black and white — dashed.

Old Photo, New Frame

OLD PHOTO, NEW FRAME

The picture shows two cousins,
Sisters,
The youngest stands beside me,

My five-year-old arms clutching
Teddy
(He's still upstairs on the shelf).

On my left shoulder sits a monkey
Wearing a sky-blue knitted jumper
Someone's granny knit

So he and his cousin could go
About town
Sharing pictures with little girls
In pleated skirts.

Staring at the worn photograph
In its sterling silver picture frame,
I'm there and I'm not.

As for the monkey,

Was he ever really there?

When I arrived home from five weeks of inter railing
I didn't have a case filled with souvenirs. Instead,
The clothes curled up inside, stank of cheap soap,
Having been washed over and over in hostel sinks,
Twice at train stations. Once, they scared away a lady
Trying to use the loo, underwear and socks all strung out
Across a set of taps. Each piece of cloth screaming *I have been.*

I've been between two men in a bus outside
Genoa, our sleeves rubbing each other up.
I've cooled as the sun dipped behind
Dracula's castle. I've shadowed the Danube at night,
All covered in dancing lights. I've rubbed carpet in prayer
In the blue mosque and stroked the Grand Bazaar.
I've moulded an old wooden bench in Thessalonica, hours
Before reaching Athens and its columns of history.
I've warmed on dry sand in Serbia, the train breaking down
An hour outside Belgrade. And I've stood on a mountain
In Zakopane, almost one piece two countries. I have been.

Now, each piece of half-washed cloth lies in a green and
Black case in a bedroom in Ireland, their future displaced.

Part Three

The Seasons

Winter is the spring of tears. And from that spring drips life.

Small Change

SMALL CHANGE

From nothing came everything:

A blank canvas, The Mona Lisa;

Cosmic change, a universe;

The seasons, new birth;

Small ideas, the spinning wheel,

Forever moving, nothing same,

And so we change beside our moon.

Winter in a Graveyard

WINTER IN A GRAVEYARD

I spent a winter in a graveyard.
The house in which I lived creaked old.
People lived there decades before both my parents
Ever born.

The man who bought the house tore up floorboards,
Put in pipes. He even made the kitchen flow
Above a basement where shackles once kept slaves.
Now it lay there, empty.

He mowed the lawn and pulled weeds from every path.
He fixed the porch and nailed each front step.

But he could do little to the backyard and its stones,
Standing anchored, some crooked but upright all the same.
And the words still read space

by

space.

Some letters weathered as if etched in felt-tipped pen.

But he couldn't rub the stones, he couldn't move them,

So I viewed them daily from my kitchen sink.

Winter Melody

WINTER MELODY

They chatter in the morn,
Brisk wings and feathers fly,
They pucker on peanuts,
Gossip as they chime.

They float and dip and dive,
Sharing thermals in the sky,
They bobble on my window,
Clearing webs and stiffened flies.

At night I hear them too,
Tucked in ditch and hedge,
Fairy tales and bed time stories,
Chirped from every ledge.

But when I wake at 2 am.,
No tree or ditch will speak,
The only sound a foreign tongue,
The one I beg to cease.

Expired

EXPIRED

Winter rain transformed my front wall:
Shapes, darkened graffiti,
Street art emerged,
Calling on the passersby.

I'd been watching a grey-bellied bird,
Before the rain came,
Before the art display.

Now the bird was gone,
So I sat and watched each brush stroke,
Puddle down my wall.

As if some old age pensioner passing up her time,
In an Art gallery on a Wintered Thursday,
Only, my ticket long expired.

Fresh Lamb

FRESH LAMB

It was a day of special deliveries.
In China, trains and buses carried people
Back from firework cities
To their patchwork green homes.

It was the start of the year of the horse
When all other animals lost rank;
Only four hooves and long manes
Would bring the happiest year,
Never mind what a groundhog would say.

But we got our own delivery that day,
When the top field of tall grass
Became a home for the first time,
Twelve brawny beige sheep
Soon springing fresh lamb.

Apprentice

APPRENTICE

Three cow lengths wide and ninety long,
Udders full of summer's song,

I walked with you, stick in hand,
Mine trailing dust and licking pats,
Yours coaxing traffic, white and black.

Your voice was strong, a single *yup*
Mine couldn't learn quite brisk enough.

Summer's Trick

SUMMER'S TRICK

Smiling faces echoed back the tractor line,
Ten whole days of summer come and almost gone,

Bales of hay multiplying from yearlong grasses
Some squared, some round, all yellowed under summer sun.

Ark like trailers tonged along short cut stalks
Tractors pronging bales onto their backs

Like some circus trick, a juggler and his bat,
Only this trick was real, summer grass to winter feed.

September Sun

SEPTEMBER SUN

Mid-September at seven fifteen:

Sun low beside my head,

Poised for her last act,

The clouds barely moving,

Watching her in awe

Waiting for her bow.

The house next door seems to stretch

Right across my couch,

Two fields over, Jimmy works in light,

His tractor churning, pulling up the soil,

Every stone now picked,

His land reborn in earth,

The sun slowly dipping, veiling it new life.

Resurrection

RESURRECTION

For Laurie Prentice

Late autumn brings casualty
To brown leaves and grey trees.
The temperature dips,
The iciest wind blows.

Saving their hearts,
Each tree bows its loosening head.
Cracked leaves,
Fingers and toes, are all shed.

Frostbite sets in,
Quickening the blow.
Glacial wind curls digits
Cast off in each breath,

Leaving bare branches
Rooted in weeping soil.
But hidden from the wind's eyes
Is the smallest beat, a heart,

For where there are tears shed,
A river flows,
And from that river ebbs spring.

Part Four

Time (the past & present)

Moving from past to present, the past often moves with us.

Suspended
SUSPENDED

Granny was the sole survivor of her past,
Her husband, her next door neighbour,
Mary B,
All gone before her down the stream of life.

And then Granny floated past,
And with her,
Her stories, token memories,
Ghost words spoken
On the fringes of another time,

Her soul trusting us
To keep her words suspended,
To pump them full of oxygen
Like bubbles of air, rooted,

In a moving stream of life.

Haunted House

HAUNTED HOUSE

A house need not be haunted
To scare the sanest mind.
Hidden in our folds lie ghosts,
Their memories unkind.

We keep them locked behind a door,
We keepers of the seal.
We live our lives away from them
As if they were not real.

Their voices rise like smoke at night,
Their chains rattle at our door,
Their laughter that of storming wind
To coax us to the floor.

Should we open up their box,
We enter to the past.
Should we travel deep enough,
They might not let us back.

Memory Leakage

MEMORY LEAKAGE

Childhood memories have a tendency

To float up

When least expected,

Like the other day,

Sitting on my bench,

I watched a dog take a leak across the road,

Observing the way he sniffed,

The way he cautiously lifted one leg,

Standing firm on the other.

When he was done

He shook his bum and

All I could think of was you

When you were ten,

Running toward your mother

Crying over something I hadn't done.

.

Standing Still

STANDING STILL

Time

Clocks

Moving

Standing still.

Clouds

Rain

Showering

Passing by.

Trees

Buds

Growing

Rainbows forming.

Eyes

Ears

Faces

Tomorrows drowning.

Aunty Daisy Dandelion

AUNTY DAISY DANDELION

During my early teenage years,
My aunt Daisy—
Well, actually, she wasn't my aunt,
She was my grandmother's sister.
But we called her Aunty Daisy Dandelion
Actually we didn't call her that
Daddy did once. And we heard him
And told her, and it stuck. Anyway,
She used to visit my granny for a week
Twice a year, summer and winter,
And I used to sit on Granny's yellowing chair
Listening to her stories of hospitals,
Matrons, and strong soldier men.
And at the end of each tale, she'd sigh
And say it was all a dream to her.
Her entire life was just a dream. And I used to laugh.
How was it possible so much could happen in one life
For it to suddenly evaporate like a cloud
On a summer's day? It's a summer's day now,
And two decades since those tales,
Daisy's voice a dream to me.
What voice will vanish next?

Toward Our Past

TOWARD OUR PAST

What if there's no future?

I mean there was a time when we were told

To believe this world was flat.

What if there's no future

And every day we wake

We step toward our past?

Ninety Minutes

NINETY MINUTES

My husband watched a soccer match on TV today.
He said it was important.
The winner took the cup.

I sat outside in the late summer air.
A cloud echoed a plane
And the wind carried a chainsaw.
There were bungee jumping birds
And tail tossing cows.
Two pheasants had a singing competition.

But when he asked what I'd done
While he watched TV
I said it wasn't important.

Three O'clock

THREE O'CLOCK

My rocking chair
Prevented me
From missing
Clocks or wares.

I sat in it
From noon
Till three,
Rocking carelessly.

I watched him
Make his lunch
And clean
Ashes from the fire.

I listened as
He hummed a tune,
"Vincent"
By Don McClean.

I spoke to him
To say goodbye

And watched
His car leave the drive,

This ritual
Keeping time —
His,
Not mine.

Nuclei

NUCLEI

Granny and Granddad

Stare at me from their wall,

My school books

Across the mahogany table.

My body shown the good room,

As if moving first class

My brain would follow

And my grades, too.

I open up biology,

The first page shows a cell,

A nucleus.

Back on the wall,

Frozen in their black and white time,

They stare

At my cells, their cells, nuclei.

Moving Past

MOVING PAST

Newspapers sit in stacks,
Yellow, faded, and once read.
The clock and sun moved on,
Yet the stack a small reminder,
When past and words were one.

Part Five

PEOPLE IN SOCIAL SETTINGS

Silence most often speaks the strongest words.

Just another Kitchen Table

She'd been a cook,
Spent years with fingers through the grill.
She knew how to bake cakes
From almost nothing.

Now, well, now she's
At my kitchen table.

I'd been in finance,
A multinational
Nine-to-five job,
Figures and numbers
Squared in my brain.

Now, both of us sitting
At my kitchen table,

Two women with nothing in common,
And yet
Everything that suddenly mattered

We had, we both had.

THE RESURRECTION AT THE TOP OF MY ROAD

It was the middle day, the one between
Jesus dying and rising,
When I left my box for a long hour
And sat at the top of my road.

There was a man with three children
Over from Leeds.
His wife was running the 10k.
They were on holiday, and on a whim
Found themselves between our ditches.
There were stragglers, there always are,
And so the race started after midday.

We sat at the 1k marker,
Viewing the runners, fresh and smiling
Before the other 9k kicked in.
Anne joined us with Bailey (a timid dog
With light brown hair)
And then we saw him, the race leader,
A second on his heels.
Even then
No bookie would take our bet.

More footfalls, heavy breathing, thumbs up,
Smiling faces focused on what
They were about to achieve.
We screamed words of encouragement,
Not that they needed it
(It made us feel good).

Almost 9k later
The same faces reappeared,
All red, having died
Between the ditches we didn't see,
All resurrecting before the finish line.
Determined eyes, hinging elbows, sprinting feet,
Whatever left in the reserve tank,
Pulled out, used up, spat out.

Bodies leaned against walls, sat on grass,
Guzzled drops of water, wiped foreheads,
Placed heads between shaking knees.
All smiled, all rejoiced.

And afterward I left them,
Dying on my couch, waiting for my resurrection
On Easter Sunday, or Monday,
Whenever it would come.

Displayed Conversation

DISPLAYED CONVERSATION

While waiting for a friend,
Two people catch my eye,

Both engrossed in signing
A colourful display.

When suddenly the Earth, it shifts —
They centre of the core.

Leaving my words, my sounds
Redundant viewers of their world.

THE ANNUAL POINT TO POINT RACES

Like the wardrobe to Narnia,
I stepped foot through a ditch,

My father's land transported
With four other fields

To the yell of *Go on!*
And jockeys at speed.

There were fences mile high
Stuffed with birch and furze green,

There were bookies in stalls
Calling bets to their doors.

There were boots, blackened mud,
And the smell of horse sweat.

At the sound of each bell,
The jocks mounted up

While kids chewed on gum

And adults gnawed luck.

Then late in the day
When the sun hit the field

The fences were gathered
And the grass returned green.

Humanitarian Aid

HUMANITARIAN AID

It is not the big names
Or deep pockets
I admire.

It's those with almost
As little as the ones
They help.

They are the ones
Who carry the weak in their
Pin sticked arms,

They share a bowl
Of watered down soup
With other

Swollen-bellied distresses.
They close the lids of the tired
To keep

The flies and shit from scratching

At their eyes. It is those
Battered

By the world,
Ignored by the world,
And yet display

Humanitarian aid,
That I most admire.

The Day My Uncle Died

THE DAY MY UNCLE DIED

For Maggie Murphy

I didn't know Gerry had passed,

But I should have.

On the final day of Donal's leave,

We travelled the grass road,

Past lambs and calves

On their three o'clock break,

The old holding the young,

The young cradling the old.

Past the golf course, before the T junction,

We came to a stop

At the garden centre.

Leafing our way past old shrubs,

New trees, the ground opened up,

And the sky poured with rain.

(We holed up in the tiny front shop).

To my left sat bottles of spray,

Enough to put out a lifetime of flies,
And to my right, pink and white wreaths
All gathered neatly to step on a grave.

When the rain cleared the sky
We picked out our flowers,
Five sets—all capable of life and her moods—
And two willow trees.
Heads bowed,
We helped them into our car.

Before travelling home,
We stopped for some petrol, it was then
I really should have known.
Donal left me to pay for our dues
And a long black car pulled up to my side,
A dead person fastened inside.

Pulling my eyes away from such loss,
A second hearse hit me, both eyes:
Alone in our car, waiting for home,
Two weeping willows
Across our back seat—
I should have known
It was the day my uncle died.

HAPPY TROUBLES

People gape under furrowed
Frowning brow, asking me how hell is.
Smiling back at them, *fine* is my reply.

Another speaks of how they'd surely drown
If they were me. Funny what we think,
All together watching, yet different views

Are had. Some upstairs looking down,
More outside looking in, while I, inside,
Forever looking out, my world of me,

Happy with the clanking chains.
Most are shocked happy is a word
I use to call myself, doubting

The workings of my mind.
Smiling, I inquire
How their troubles be.

Ghost Estate

GHOST ESTATE

Every sixth day about noon
He threw me onto his shoulders,
Smelling of cows and their dung.

I sat on top of the world, sucking
In him and the fields, grasping
And tugging at trees, listening

To him and his tales, leprechauns
Loose in the fields. Locking in
Those around dawn, veiling

Gates from their eyes, vanishing
Gaps to escape. Laughing
And yelping at him, we kicked

Our way through the fields,
The very same fields now filled
With houses and concrete debris.

Perhaps they'd throw away keys

Should leprechauns return
To these fields?

Introverted Words

INTRODUCTED WORDS

Voices in awkward
Social events
Are
Birds,
Searching
For a mate.
Dogs marking out their post—

Nervous chatter,
Hiding
Shaking hands,
Frenzied minds
Spewing
Thoughtless words,

Talking much of
Almost
Nothing.

Sitting in my corner
Veiled
In silent silence,
I respect the words.

The Big Spread

THE BIG SPREAD

They laid her out in the good room
Amongst the cups and china plates
That watched from layers of rubbed down glass.

They placed twelve seats against two walls,
Six on either side, two cartons of un-cracked eggs.
They placed her where the sun faced best.

And at her head, they lay a daffodil,
It's smooth leaves a reminder of her past.
And when the neighbours called

They bowed their heads,
Knowing how they treated her best.

What is it to be Normal?

WHAT IS IT TO BE NORMAL?

What is it to be normal?

Is it caring what they think?

Doing what they expect?

Is normal filling houses with things

So magpies can inspect?

Is normal playing make believe,

Being someone you pretend?

Is normal watching what you say

For fear of being rejected?

Is normal wanting to conform

Just to be accepted?

Well, listen now, I take this oath

And to Abnormal Valley go!

After Thought

This book was inspired by a habit of mine: watching the seasons drift from my garden bench. My addiction has become so excessive, I can be found during late autumn and winter, wrapped in a hat, scarf and coat, more layers than the most exuberant wedding cake!

The bench has gifted me blooming flowers, mating hares, a family of pheasants who use my front garden as a short cut between two fields, and, of course, my small garden birds who glide and bounce onto their feeder daily. My summer observatory also spies on three families of house martins, on holiday from Africa. They enjoy swooping just above my head, their white bellies grazing the top of my forehead. Luckily, because I sit as still as I do, a wagtail enjoys propping himself beside my bench almost daily. Occasionally nature throws me an obscure treat. Such as the one I enjoyed on Wednesday June 11th, 2014, a day I will forever remember, when a sparrowhawk astutely set his wings into flight nearby. As you know, there were no casualties.

Observing is what I do. I love to watch, think, listen, and just be. There is nothing more soothing than the sound of my silent body wrapped in nature's chorus.

Thank you for stopping by and sharing my bench. Now, go and sit, walk, listen, watch, observe, inhale this world of ours. Let your pores soak up its sounds, colour, and smell. Until next time, *slán go fóill (until next time}*

www.mariehcurran.com

Bio

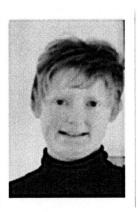

Marie Hanna Curran holds a degree in Equine Science from the University of Limerick, Ireland and lives in rural Galway with her husband and many wild birds. Due to illness, she is currently housebound, however ME/CFS – Myalgic Encephalomyelitis - doesn't stop her writing. She believes writing is soul food and such food must be shared. Two of her poems appeared in *The Galway Review* and seven pieces of work weaved their way between the pages of the published anthology *Poems from Conflicted Hearts* (Tayen Lane Publishing, 2014). Her articles concerning illness and anti-bullying were published in Irish newspapers and her feature against bullying was read on radio. Her thoughts can also be found in the magazine *Athenry News and Views*.